Those Loving Feelings

Those Loving Feelings

The Song of Solomon for Newlyweds

JOHN R. GUNN

WESTBOW
P R E S S
A DIVISION OF THOMAS NELSON

WestBow Press books may be ordered through booksellers or by contacting:
WestBow Press
A Division of Thomas Nelson
1663 Liberty Drive
Bloomington, IN 47403
www.westbowpress.com
1-(866) 928-1240

ISBN: 978-1-4497-7508-7 (e)
ISBN: 978-1-4497-7509-4 (sc)
ISBN: 978-1-4497-7510-0 (hc)
Library of Congress Control Number: 2012921202
Printed in the United States of America
WestBow Press rev. date: 01/14/2013

To my wife and daughters and daughters-in-law, who, in my esteem, fulfill the ideals of womanhood embodied in this writing.

Other books by John R. Gunn

Under the Gunn: Inspiration for Preachers

Be the Best at Who You Are: 75
Life-Shaping Bible Proverbs

John R. Gunn (1877–1956) was first a minister and then a daily newspaper columnist inspiring readers for over thirty-six years. After his death, his columns, were reprinted daily by popular demand for fifteen more years. His messages had broad interdenominational appeal, and became two-and-a-half-minute radio scripts for broadcast over 2,000 radio stations, plus the Armed Forces Radio Network. This inspirational program, *Be Still and Know*, was produced by the Protestant Radio and Television Center of Atlanta. Its president proclaimed in 1972, "Certainly no one person has contributed so much to this program, which has been on the air for some fourteen years." Today, Gunn's work can be read and heard on the Day1.org website.

Contents

ACKNOWLEDGMENTS

Without the encouragement and outstanding assistance of Emily Cooper of Clifton, New Jersey, and Dan L. Vant Kerkhoff of Hudsonville, Michigan, this book would not have been published. Their generous contribution to the editing of this book is gratefully acknowledged.

INTRODUCTION

If you've recently wed, or if you are about to: Congratulations! On the big day that you "become one," your new bond is joyfully announced at the ceremony and celebrated by your family and friends at the reception. It launches the two of you on a journey with the promised perks of lifelong love, romance, and deepening friendship.

Marriage is universal throughout our human history of diverse cultures and traditions. At the start, it was mandated by our Creator. "Male and female he created them. God blessed them and said to them, 'Be fruitful and increase in number'" (Genesis 1:27–29).

God did not merely command them to get married and have children; he instilled his human creatures with feelings of physical attraction, love, and passion to make it happen. He wired us for sexuality, one of the strongest forces we can encounter. On your marital adventure, biblical guidelines will challenge and equip you to take the high road by fortifying and nourishing your love and passion within the solid walls of commitment and loyalty to each other, to yourself, and to your God.

To this end, the chapters of this book explore that unrivaled composition of ancient erotic literature, the Song of Solomon. To the surprise of some, it is part of the Hebrew Scriptures. Rich in symbolic references to male and female attributes, its cadences portray a supremely beautiful love that bonds man and woman through the phases of attraction, courtship, intimacy, conflict, further romance, and commitment through marriage. The pair, in turn, converse in poetic dialogue.

Some interpreters have downplayed these pleasurable images of human love by asserting that the Song of Solomon depicts God's love for Israel, or later on, Christ's love for His church. But the original intent of this work can't be camouflaged. Its passages comprise a magnificent and significant source of instruction and inspiration for lovers that is as relevant today as it was centuries ago. The Song of Solomon for all time exemplifies the truth that between a man and a woman committed to each other, love's flame not only ignites, but also flourishes and endures.

James R. Gunn

CHAPTER ONE
Love Thrives on Confidence and Trust

Solomon's Song of Songs.

She ★

Let him kiss me with the kisses of his mouth—

    for your love is more delightful than wine.

Pleasing is the fragrance of your perfumes;

    your name is like perfume poured out.

    No wonder the young women love you!

Take me away with you—let us hurry!

    Let the king bring me into his chambers.

★   The main male and female speakers (identified primarily on the basis of the gender of the relevant Hebrew forms) are indicated by the captions "He" and "She" respectively. The words of others are marked "Friends." In some instances, the divisions and their captions are debatable.

John R. Gunn

Friends

We rejoice and delight in you;

> *we will praise your love more than wine.*

She

How right they are to adore you!

—Song of Solomon 1:1-4

The Song of Solomon is a song of triumph in love and marriage. It consists of a collection of songs or lyrics, and its objectives are to teach us the sacredness of human love and to elevate our thinking about the function of marriage.

The first lyric sings of love's fulfillment—the fulfillment that comes when romance has flowered into a state of marriage and love is sure. The bride speaks: in her thoughts, she enthrones the bridegroom as her king. Musing upon the king's love and her new experience in his chambers as his bride, she breaks out in a soliloquy. She first expresses her bridal joy over the king's kisses and love: "Let him kiss me with the kisses of his mouth—for your love is more delightful than wine." She could, naturally, be jealous of the virgins in the company of the king, but she doesn't mind them. If they love the king, their presence is something to be expected: "Pleasing is the fragrance of your perfumes; your name is like perfume poured out. No wonder the young women love you!" She finds her chief joy and delight not in the luxurious chambers where the king brings her, nor in the rare wine served by his cupbearers, but in his person and his love: "Take me away with you—let us hurry! Let the king bring me into his chambers. We rejoice and delight in you; we will praise your love more than wine." She sees no reason to be concerned if the king finds pleasure in the company of the virgins. In her thoughts, she places their love for him above suspicion: "No wonder the young women love you!"

In his poem, "Venus and Adonis," Shakespeare writes, "Where Love reigns, disturbing Jealousy doth call himself Affection's sentinel." In contrast, here in the Song of Solomon is an affection that requires no guarding by that sentinel; it is a love so sure that it leaves no place for distrust, nor for the doubts and suspicions that spring from jealousy.

In England, during mediaeval times, a girl customarily led the bridal party scattering flowers along their way. How sad, to leave the flowers of romance to wither on the path until they have no more beauty or life. It is a high moment when the bride and groom stand before the marriage altar and vow to love and cherish each other "until death us do part." Think of the radiance of love and hope that fills the sky from horizon to horizon. Think of the future years of life-enriching comradeship and domestic felicity promised by that union. Then, think of how frequently marriages that began so happily and promised so much end tragically. Sad, isn't it?

Why is it that so many marriages fail? There are many causes, but a common one is jealousy. Often, there is no basis to it besides low self-esteem. Love feeds on confidence and trust, whereas jealousy feeds on doubt and rumor, and "rumor doth double, like the voice and echo," as Shakespeare writes.

Jealousy is a green-eyed monster you must immediately trample and never allow a chance to invade the sanctity of your home. Above all, never give occasion for jealousy. Think of the infamy of breaking of the marriage bond. Consider what a tragedy divorce is—it means bidding farewell to the heart's dreams as uttered in the words, "until death us do part." It is the burial of an ideal, and the saddest death in all the world.

Often a husband or wife sues for divorce on the grounds of incompatibility. Recall the Old Testament parable in which "a thistle in Lebanon sent a message to a cedar in Lebanon, 'Give your daughter to my son in marriage'" (2 Kings 14:9). The thistle and cedar are different plants with nothing in common, no compatibility. A couple contemplating marriage should consider very carefully whether they are temperamentally suited to each other, whether they can walk together agreeably, whether their ideals blend, and whether they can harmonize their personalities and their aims.

The Cherokee Indians have an impressive marriage ceremony. The man and woman join hands over running water to indicate that their lives will henceforth flow in one stream.

A thistle-and-cedar marriage promises no good to either the one or the other. There can be no real or helpful partnership between a man and woman who are as wide apart as these two plants of the forest. The result would be unrealized ideals, disappointment, unhappiness, and incompatibility—a miserable mess.

Marriage calls for mutual fitness as well as an adjustment period. Two opposite natures may learn to adapt to one another when there is mutual love, but it is a difficult thing to achieve, and it requires earnest resolve and mutual effort. The appropriate time to consider the probabilities is before marriage, not afterwards.

Marriage should be a matter of prayer. It is too sacred and holy a union to enter into without first seeking divine guidance.

CHAPTER TWO
The Heart Reflects the Highest Beauty

She

Dark am I, yet lovely,

    daughters of Jerusalem,

    dark like the tents of Kedar,

    like the tent curtains of Solomon.

Do not stare at me because I am dark,

    because I am darkened by the sun.

My mother's sons were angry with me

    and made me take care of the vineyards;

    my own vineyard I had to neglect.

—Song of Solomon 1:5-6

The speaker is the bride.

Obviously, she was a country girl. The daughters of Jerusalem, observing that she was rustic and unschooled in the graces of social life, wondered what the bridegroom saw in her to win his love and induce him to make her his bride. Sensing this, she speaks. She cannot disavow her origin. The sun scorched her because she was working to tend the family vineyards. Her swarthiness comes of toil. She did not tend to her own personal graces and charms because of her sacrifice for her family. She does not apologize in the sense of confessing failure; her apology has the sense of defense. Tending the vineyards meant sacrificing something of her personal charms, but it was a sacrifice she made willingly and gladly for the sake of family.

This is something we often see: a young woman denying herself the things all young women crave in order to take care of her aging parents or to help provide for younger brothers and sisters. What a noble sacrifice!

The daughters of Jerusalem might wonder at the bridegroom's love of this simple country maiden who bears what they consider marks of limitation or lack of beauty. Her marks of sunburn and swarthiness are the evidence of what he values in her. He sees them as symbols of the truest beauty.

The greatest beauty in women is of personality and character rather than social grace or physicality. Beauty is a subtle thing. It is not dependent upon facial proportion; it can be seen in the most irregular features. What makes one really beautiful is the soul shining through the face.

Cultivate in your heart the spirit of meekness, gentleness, and modesty, and your face will shine with a beauty that far surpasses superficial beauty. The immortal poet Johann Schiller said, "Modest humility is beauty's crown."

A graceful figure and lovely face are admirable gifts, but without corresponding grace and good qualities of heart, they lose much of their charm. Purity of mind and heart grant the greatest beauty. Womanly grace and refinement of character are women's crowning attractive qualities. "It should be that of your inner self, the unfading beauty of a gentle and quiet spirit, which is of great worth in God's sight" (1 Peter 3:4).

CHAPTER THREE
Whether Castle or Cottage, Paradise Is Where Love Dwells

She

Tell me, you whom I love, where you graze your flock

    and where you rest your sheep at midday.

Why should I be like a veiled woman

    beside the flocks of your friends?

Friends

If you do not know, most beautiful of women, follow

    the tracks of the sheep and graze your young goats

    by the tents of the shepherds.

He

I liken you, my darling, to a mare

> *among Pharaoh's chariot horses.*

Your cheeks are beautiful with earrings,

> *your neck with strings of jewels.*

We will make you earrings of gold, studded with silver.

She

While the king was at his table,

> *my perfume spread its fragrance.*

My beloved is to me a sachet of myrrh resting between my breasts.

> *My beloved is to me a cluster of henna blossoms*

> *from the vineyards of En Gedi.*

He

How beautiful you are, my darling!

> *Oh, how beautiful! Your eyes are doves.*

She

How handsome you are, my beloved!

> *Oh, how charming! And our bed is verdant.*

He

The beams of our house are cedars; our rafters are firs.

—Song of Solomon 1:7-17

This song is a dialogue between two lovers about to be married. In the first lines, they are arranging a tryst where the flocks feed under cover of the shepherd's tent. In their conversation at this romantic rendezvous, they address each other with endearing terms, the suitor calling her "my darling" and the maiden calling him "my beloved." Their romance has reached the stage in which they pledge their love to each other.

The dialogue that follows is tender and beautiful. It is highly visual and poetic with the fine spirit of the East. Anticipating the day when his love will be his queen, the lover compares his betrothed to a steed pulling Pharaoh's chariot and declares, "We will make you earrings of gold, studded with silver." In her reply, she ignores his reference to the rich gifts he proposes to lavish upon her, and says simply, "My beloved is to me a sachet of myrrh … a cluster of henna blossoms," as if to say he himself fulfills all that she desires, and she doesn't need golden earrings studded with silver. Satisfied with him and content with his love, she cares not for regal splendor. A simple life and simple things fulfill her ideal. She will make him her king and sit at his table, letting her "perfume spread its fragrance." It is her ambition to bring to the table of her king a personality and a womanly grace that will send forth a sweet savor like perfume. It would be a happy occasion for any king, and for his kingdom, to have the royal table graced by such a queen.

Now the lover, perceiving the significance of the simplicity of her speech, takes her cue and uses simple speech to speak of her: "How beautiful you are, my darling! Oh, how beautiful! Your eyes are doves." Responding with like praise for him, she once again expresses her desire for a simple life and simple things: "Our bed is verdant. The beams of our house are cedars; our rafters are firs." She has no dreams of palatial chambers; she is content to dwell with him in a plain house like one of the shepherd's tents, with its bed of green, beams of cedar, and rafters of fir.

Paradise is always where love dwells, even if that dwelling-place is only a shepherd's tent. Without love, a palace is no more than a prison.

In a corner of a window of old Astley Castle, one can see the faint lines scratched by a woman's diamond: "My prison!" What a tragedy in those words! They were scratched by Lady Jane Grey. Titles, lands, maids of honor, dresses, jewels, and a thousand other such rich gifts were hers. Yet, because the sweet attention of love was missing from that palace, she was like a bird beating its wings against the bars of an iron cage.

No palace was ever beautiful enough, no royal wine quaffed from vessels of gold was ever sweet enough to satisfy the heart of a woman starving for the heavenly manna of love. Solomon observes, "Better is a dinner of herbs where love is, than a stalled ox and hatred therewith" (Proverb 15:17). Where love is, the plainest house is sweet with heaven, and plainest bread is heavenly manna.

In his play *Comus,* John Milton writes of concern and courtesy that they are "sooner found in lowly sheds with smoky rafters, than in tapestry halls, and courts of princes." Love warms the barest, humblest home with tender care, and make it radiant with selfless ministry. From countless thousands of simple "houses with beams of cedar and rafters of fir," there is witness that the woman in this song is right in her conception of happy wedded life. Not riches, nor luxuries, nor rich meats, nor sweet wines, but mutual love is the crown of wedded bliss. Better to live in a "lowly shed with smoky rafters" with love than a palatial mansion where love is missing.

CHAPTER FOUR
May the Love-flag over You Ever Wave

She

I am a rose of Sharon, a lily of the valleys.

He

Like a lily among thorns is my

darling among the young women.

She

Like an apple tree among the trees of the forest

is my beloved among the young men.

I delight to sit in his shade,

and his fruit is sweet to my taste.

Let him lead me to the banquet hall,

and let his banner over me be love.

Strengthen me with raisins, refresh me

  with apples, for I am faint with love.

His left arm is under my head,

  and his right arm embraces me.

      —Song of Solomon 2:1-6

The bride speaks first, describing herself as a rose and a lily. The lily referred to is a scarlet flower that grew profusely in the valleys of Palestine. The rose is a white crocus, a common flower that abounded in the region known as the Plain of Sharon. She does not say "the rose of Sharon" or "the lily of the valleys," as it appears in the King James Version; rather, her words in the American Standard Version and the New International Version read, "a rose of Sharon" and "a lily of the valleys." Her description of herself is modest—she sees nothing in her own person or beauty that is out of the ordinary.

In response, the bridegroom accepts her description of herself as a lily—not as one among many, but as one who, in his eyes, makes all others look like thorns. This is the outlook of true love. To the true lover, the object of his love is the most beautiful of women. Her days of toil may have left its marks upon her, but to him, they are beauty marks that no beauty shop could duplicate.

After this dialogue, the bride, speaking as though to herself, continues: "I delight to sit in his shade, and his fruit is sweet to my taste. Let him lead me to the banquet hall, and let his banner over me be love. His left arm is under my head, and his right arm embraces me."

She desires nothing more than to sit under the shadow of her beloved and feed upon his love and companionship. She feels at ease under the banner of his love. It is enough for her to be in his embrace, to feel his strong hands supporting her; to know that he is hers and she is his.

What a beautiful thing this is: two lovers so passionate for each other that there is no room for anyone to come between them, and so completely satisfied with each other that nothing else matters. Any couple who feels love as truly as this can look forward to a happy and successful marriage.

CHAPTER FIVE
Little Foxes Can Ruin a Vineyard

She

Listen! My beloved! Look! Here he comes,

    leaping across the mountains, bounding over the hills.

My beloved is like a gazelle or a young stag.

    Look! There he stands behind our wall,

    gazing through the windows, peering through the lattice.

My beloved spoke and said to me, "Arise, my darling,

    my beautiful one, come with me.

See! The winter is past; the rains are over and gone.

    Flowers appear on the earth; the season of singing

    has come, the cooing of doves is heard in our land.

The fig tree forms its early fruit; the

blossoming vines spread their fragrance.

Arise, come, my darling; my beautiful one, come with me."

He

My dove in the clefts of the rock,

in the hiding places on the mountainside,

show me your face, let me hear your voice;

for your voice is sweet, and your face is lovely.

Catch for us the foxes, the little foxes that ruin

the vineyards, our vineyards that are in bloom.

She

My beloved is mine and I am his; he browses among the lilies.

Until the day breaks and the shadows flee,

turn, my beloved, and be like a gazelle or

like a young stag on the rugged hills.

—Song of Solomon 2:8-17

In this dialogue, a suitor and a maiden have pledged their love and are now awaiting their wedding day. This scene could well have inspired Shakespeare's window scene in *Romeo and Juliet*, Act II, scene ii.

ROMEO
But soft! what light through yonder window breaks?
It is the east, and Juliet is the sun.

It is my lady, O, it is my love!

The brightness of her cheek would shame those stars
As daylight doth a lamp.
See, how she leans her cheek upon her hand!
O, that I were a glove upon that hand,
That I might touch that cheek!

JULIET
O, Romeo, Romeo!

How camest thou hither, tell me, and wherefore?
The orchard walls are high and hard to climb,
and the place death ...
If any of my kinsmen find thee here.

ROMEO
With love's light wings did I o'er-perch these walls;
For stony limits cannot hold love out,
And what love can do that dares love attempt;
Therefore thy kinsmen are no let to me.

On and on, their discourse of love goes, until at last, Juliet lovingly warns him.

JULIET
'Tis almost morning; I would have thee gone:
And yet no farther than a wanton's bird;
Who lets it hop a little from her hand,
And with a silk thread plucks it back again,

ROMEO
I would I were thy bird.
JULIET
Sweet, so would I:
Yet I should kill thee with much cherishing.
Good night, good night! parting is such
sweet sorrow,
That I shall say good night till it be morrow.

The window scene of our song takes place at the maiden's home, in the garden just beneath her bedchamber. Like any young woman engaged to be married, this maiden is counting the hours to the next visit by her lover. One night, in the quiet of her chamber, she hears a voice, and excitedly utters, "Listen! My beloved!" She knows that voice and senses what it signals: "Look! Here he comes." In her imagination, she hears the rhythm of pounding feet as he comes, "leaping across the mountains, bounding over the hills. My beloved is like a gazelle or a young stag. Look! There he stands behind our wall, gazing through the windows, peering through the lattice." She waits and listens, and presently hears him calling, "Arise, my darling, my beautiful one, come with me."

In the next lines, he presses his appeal. The season is favorable, he tells her: "See! The winter is past; the rains are over and gone. Flowers appear on the earth; the season of singing has come, the cooing of doves is heard in our land. The fig tree forms its early fruit; the blossoming vines spread their fragrance."

Then, again, he calls her. "Arise, come, my darling; my beautiful one, come with me." In tense eagerness he awaits her answer, and the wall of her house towers before him like the wall of a steep cliff. Standing there framed in the high window, she seems hidden in "the clefts of the rock, in the hiding places on the mountainside," so he cries, "Show me your face, let me hear your voice."

Her answer is beautiful and meaningful: "Catch for us the foxes, the little foxes that ruin the vineyards, our vineyards that are in bloom. My beloved is mine and I am his; he browses among the lilies. Until the day breaks and the shadows flee, turn, my beloved, and be like a gazelle or like a young stag on the rugged hills."

There are "mountains of separation" between them. She cannot come away with him; for the time being they must maintain a proper distance. Meanwhile, let him guard the vineyard of their love. She is saying, "We must wait awhile, but let us keep the vineyard of our love pristine, let us guard its tender grapes from the foxes of doubt, suspicion, and jealousy. Let us be assured and content in the knowledge that we belong to each other. Until the day we have promised ourselves shall come, go back to the hills and to your flock. However long the time until the day breaks and the shadows flee, remember: "My beloved is mine and I am his."

Their marriage will not be a hasty one; their love is the real thing, and it can stand the test of waiting. I have known many cases in which a test of this kind would have helped the parties concerned.

CHAPTER SIX

To Appreciate Your Love, Imagine It Lost

She

All night long on my bed I looked for the one my heart loves;

I looked for him but did not find him.

I will get up now and go about the city,

through its streets and squares; I will search

for the one my heart loves. So I looked

for him but did not find him.

The watchmen found me as they made their rounds

in the city. "Have you seen the one my heart loves?"

Scarcely had I passed them when I found the one my heart loves.

I held him and would not let him go till

I had brought him to my mother's house,

to the room of the one who conceived me.

—Song of Solomon 3:1-4

A young woman in love thought in her dreams she had lost her beloved, and still dreaming, she rises up and goes into the city, searching for him in the streets. At first her search is fruitless, but at last she finds him, holds him, and will not let him go.

This poetically describes love when it masters a life. A lover can even imagine that one's beloved could be lost. This fear may be subconscious in daytime but more readily perceived at night.

This interpretation of love can start one thinking of the difference which the presence or absence of love makes in one's life. The way love changes one's disposition is both marvelous and essentially positive. If you love no one besides yourself, your selfish spirit will dominate your behavior and conduct, creating a vain, sensitive, critical, grouchy, and resentful disposition. Such a disposition destroys the peace and pleasure of any company a person may have. Love reverses the traits and dispositions created by such selfishness.

In his essay, "On Falling in Love," F.W. Boreham writes of an well-known concert pianist who one day offered advice to a younger musician. The young man was a brilliant performer and his technique was flawless, but he had an aloof, taciturn disposition. His heart had never been warmed by any intimate friendship, so there was a coldness in his playing which the older and more experienced musician easily discerned. "Will you let me tell you, my boy, that your playing lacks one thing. So far," she said to him, "you have missed the greatest thing in the world. And unless you fall in love, there will always be a certain cold perfection about your music. Unless you come to love another human being passionately and unselfishly, you will never touch human hearts as deeply as you might."

Nothing makes life so interesting as being in love with someone. Not until you fall in love will life yield to you its sweetest pleasures and purest joys. Not until we are mastered by passionate love for another can we live a life that is full, abundant, and beautiful.

CHAPTER SEVEN
The Wedding Event Must Never Be Trivialized

She

Who is this coming up from the wilderness like a

        column of smoke, perfumed with myrrh and incense

        made from all the spices of the merchant?

Look! It is Solomon's carriage, escorted by sixty warriors,

        the noblest of Israel, all of them wearing the sword,

        all experienced in battle, each with his sword at his

        side, prepared for the terrors of the night.

King Solomon made for himself the carriage;

        he made it of wood from Lebanon.

Its posts he made of silver, its base of gold. Its seat was

        upholstered with purple, its interior inlaid with love.

Daughters of Jerusalem, Come out, and look, you daughters

of Zion. Look on King Solomon wearing a crown,

the crown with which his mother crowned him

on the day of his wedding, the day his heart rejoiced.

—Song of Solomon 3:6-11

This is the scene witnessed by the daughters of Zion when they go forth to behold the bridegroom: he is wearing the crown his mother crowned him with, and the bridal train approaches the place where the his wedding ceremony and feast will be held. No account is given of these proceedings, but from the richness and stateliness of the procession the song describes, we may be sure nothing is wanting to make the occasion impressive and marked with dignity and solemnity—just as so sacred an event should be.

Since that day in the early dawn of creation when the first marriage was solemnized by God Himself, marriage has been a sacred and holy act to be solemnized in the sight of God. It is entirely fitting to enter into marriage joyously; the wedding day is naturally one of joyfulness and exultation. However, it is not a day for frivolity—to make it so would be to make a mockery of the most sacred act of human life. If a wedding is something to be solemnized in the sight of God, it is certainly not an occasion for riotous levity. It should be set amid religious associations and marked with befitting dignity.

Many marriages these days are scandalized rather than solemnized. Often couples seek novel means of getting married to shock their friends or make a sensation. One wonders if we are losing reverence for things sacred. We are too given to facetiousness in the presence of the sanctities of life. Some people attach every possible suggestion of levity to sacred things, particularly marriage. Too many "celebrity marriages" quickly dissolve. This holy ordnance is used to promote personal publicity. They forget that marriage is the door into one of life's deepest mysteries.

Marriage was never treated lightly in Israel, which gave the world this song of triumph in love and marriage. In the Jewish betrothal ceremony, the groom gives the bride a piece of money and a parchment on which both their names are written, and repeats before witnesses the sacred words, "Lo, you are betrothed to me." Together they share a cup of wine, the sacramental seal of their promises, and then bow their heads to the solemn cadence of the benediction: "Blessed art thou, O Lord our God, King of the world, who hath sanctified us by His commandments ... Blessed art Thou, who sanctifiest Israel by marriage and betrothal."

CHAPTER EIGHT
Tell Her How Beautiful She Is

He

How beautiful you are, my darling!

 Oh, how beautiful! Your eyes behind your veil are doves.

Your hair is like a flock of goats descending

 from the hills of Gilead.

Your teeth are like a flock of sheep just shorn,

 coming up from the washing. Each has its twin;

 not one of them is alone.

Your lips are like a scarlet ribbon; your mouth is lovely.

 Your temples behind your veil are like the halves of a pomegranate.

Your neck is like the tower of David, built with courses

 of stone; on it hang a thousand shields,

all of them shields of warriors.

Your breasts are like two fawns, like twin fawns

of a gazelle that browse among the lilies.

Until the day breaks and the shadows flee,

I will go to the mountain of myrrh and to the hill of incense.

—Song of Solomon 4:1-6

Sung by the bridegroom to his bride, his song underscores her bridal loveliness and expresses his delight in her. The imagery he employs in describing her person and personality paints an exquisite picture of her health, freshness, and natural beauty; of grace and loveliness combined with strength, and blended with the finest qualities of womanhood.

Some commentators think that this bridegroom was King Solomon. Whether or not that is true, this is a bride who might well grace a king's court. Her scarlet lips and comely speech befit a queen; her character and personality would make her a tower of strength in a royal household of mighty men.

She would not appear out of place in the court of King Solomon. She fulfills the ideal of beauty which the king of Scotland perceives in Ellen of Loch Katrine in Sir Walter Scott's poem "The Lady of the Lake":

> And ne'er did Grecian chisel trace
> A Nymph, a Naiad, or a Grace,
> Of finer form or lovelier face!
> What though the sun, with ardent frown,
> Had slightly tinged her cheek with brown,—
>
> What though no rule of courtly grace
> To measured mood had trained her pace,—
>
> What though upon her speech there hung
> The accents of the mountain tongue.

In Alfred Lord Tennyson's poem "Lancelot and Elaine," young Lavaine proposes a venture to win a certain diamond for Elaine, to which Sir Torre remarks, "A fair large diamond, such be for queens, and not for simple maids." Seeing Elaine flush at this disparagement, Lancelot speaks up, saying, "If what is fair be but for what is fair, and only queens are to be counted so, then my judgment must be rash, for I think this maid might wear as fair a jewel as there is on earth without violating the rule that like should only be joined with like."

In this passage Tennyson is saying that any simple maid who fulfills the ideal of true beauty in women—beauty of spirit and character—could wear apparel befitting a queen without any mark of incongruity, nor would there be incongruity were she made a queen amid regal splendor. This is true of the bride in song. She possesses a personality and soul that qualify her to wear a queen's crown without violating the rule that like should only be joined with like.

CHAPTER NINE
Your Love for Each Other Is a Private Garden

He

You are altogether beautiful, my darling;

    there is no flaw in you.

Come with me from Lebanon, my bride, come with me

    from Lebanon. Descend from the crest of Amana,

    from the top of Senir, the summit of Hermon,

    from the lions' dens and the mountain haunts of leopards.

You have stolen my heart, my sister, my bride;

    you have stolen my heart with one glance of your

    eyes, with one jewel of your necklace.

How delightful is your love, my sister, my bride!

    How much more pleasing is your love than wine,

and the fragrance of your perfume more than any spice!

Your lips drop sweetness as the honeycomb, my bride;

milk and honey are under your tongue. The fragrance

of your garments is like the fragrance of Lebanon.

You are a garden locked up, my sister, my bride;

you are a spring enclosed, a sealed fountain.

Your plants are an orchard of pomegranates with

choice fruits, with henna and nard,

nard and saffron, calamus and cinnamon,

with every kind of incense tree, with myrrh and aloes

and all the finest spices.

You are a garden fountain, a well of flowing water

streaming down from Lebanon.

—Song of Solomon 4:7-15

This is another song sung to the bride. After expressing his delight and complete satisfaction with the bride, the bridegroom bids her come with him: "Come with me from Lebanon, my bride." A native of Lebanon, she must naturally be deeply attached to the land of her childhood and youth. If it seems a rude thing to tear her away from the place where her life is rooted, then he pleads the excuse of love: "You have stolen my heart, my sister, my bride; you have stolen my heart with one glance of your eyes." Her look of love gives him courage to ask her to come with him from Lebanon.

Will she come? What will she say? "She speaks yet she says nothing; what of that? Her eye discourses," says Romeo of Juliet. In her eyes, love speaks. When love speaks, every other voice is hushed, all else is forgotten. Whatever is left behind, whether city or country, whether palace or cabin, love says, "Where you go I will go, and where you stay I will stay. Your people will be my people and your God my God. Where you die I will die, and there I will be buried. May the Lord deal with me, be it ever so severely, if even death separates you and me" (Ruth 1:16–17).

We might call special attention to the couplet in which the bridegroom speaks of the bride as "a garden locked up, a spring enclosed, a sealed fountain"—a beautiful and delicate metaphor for the bride's virginity, a precious thing she has kept in pristine purity. She is a woman, but she still has the bloom of girlhood about her. You may have noticed before what is called "bloom" on peaches and plums: it is a white haze on the surface, and its beauty is so delicate that even a little careless handling mars it. Once marred, it can never again be the way it was. Innocent girlhood has a beautiful, precious bloom unlike anything else in the world; this bloom later becomes the glory of virtuous womanhood. It is so delicate that it will not bear careless handling. In this couplet, the poet seems to be saying to very young girls, "Permit no profane hand to touch that precious, delicate bloom. Allow no unholy handling of it. Permit no vulgar intruders to invade the defenses of that innocent delicacy which nature has placed around your person. If you attain to an honorable and happy womanhood, guard your girlhood and keep it like an enclosed garden, like a sealed fountain."

CHAPTER TEN
Love Blends Passion and Purity

She

Awake, north wind, and come, south wind!

> *Blow on my garden, that its fragrance*
>
> *may spread everywhere. Let my beloved*
>
> *come into his garden and taste its choice fruits.*

He

I have come into my garden, my sister, my bride;

> *I have gathered my myrrh with my spice.*
>
> *I have eaten my honeycomb and my honey;*
>
> *I have drunk my wine and my milk.*

John R. Gunn

Friends

Eat, friends, and drink; drink your fill of love.

—Song of Solomon 4:16; 5:1

In the first part of this poem, the bride is speaking. She remembers the song the bridegroom sang to her when he asked her to come with him from Lebanon—how he sang of her as "an orchard of pomegranates with choice fruits, with henna and nard, with every kind of incense tree, with myrrh and aloes and all the finest spices." The dominant desire of her heart is to fulfill his expectations; she wants to be all that he anticipates. She thinks of herself, her personality, as her garden. She now belongs to him; she is his garden. Will he find her to be the garden he thought her to be? What a tragic thing it would be for both of them if he were disappointed in her! Musing on this, she is moved to cry, "Awake, north wind, and come, south wind! Blow on my garden, that its fragrance may spread everywhere." She is thinking of her beloved, not herself—not about whether he will satisfy her, but whether she will satisfy him. Her desire is that the fragrance of her personality will flow forth for his sake. Therefore, she calls the north and south winds to blow upon her garden. This image is poetic. The cold wind from the north is the spirit of purity. The warm wind from the south is the spirit of passion. Under this double ministry, the beauty of personality will be perfected, purity will be suffused with passion, and passion will be governed by purity. After uttering this, she quietly adds, "Let my beloved come into his garden and taste its choice fruits."

In the next lines, the bridegroom speaks. As if assuring her that she is indeed the garden he expected, and that she completely answers his desires, he declares, "I have come into my garden, my sister, my bride; I have gathered my myrrh with my spice. I have eaten my honeycomb and my honey; I have drunk my wine and my milk." At this point, a well-wisher says, "Eat, friends, and drink; drink your fill of love." This is a beautiful and tender scene: the wedded lovers hold sweet communion and drink of each other's love.

In this scene, the bride and bridegroom stand at the threshold of wedded life. The bride sees nothing unholy in marital desire. She expects to yield herself to the bridegroom in marital love. In contemplation of this, she prays that the love she gives him shall be warm and suffused with a pure spirit. She feels no sense of shame or weakness as she faces the issue of marriage. Why should conjugal love be thought of with shame or weakness? It is a great mystery and a great necessity that lies at the foundation of human existence, morality, and happiness.

The poet has none of the false modesty that shrouds this mystery in secrecy. The principal intent of this great poem is to elevate our thinking of the function of marriage. Many see in the poem a mystical symbolism; they interpret the description of the connection between a man and a woman as depicting the relationship between Jehovah and Israel, or the union between Christ and the church. These may be acceptable secondary interpretations, but the poem is primarily an expression of pure marital love as ordained by God, and a vindication that marital love is neither ascetic nor lustful.

CHAPTER ELEVEN
The Loving Heart Stays Alert

She

I slept but my heart was awake. Listen! My beloved is knocking:

> *"Open to me, my sister, my darling, my dove, my*
>
> *flawless one. My head is drenched with dew,*
>
> *my hair with the dampness of the night."*

I have taken off my robe—must I put it on again? I have

> *washed my feet—must I soil them again?*

My beloved thrust his hand through the latch-opening;

> *my heart began to pound for him.*

I arose to open for my beloved, and my hands

> *dripped with myrrh, my fingers with flowing myrrh,*
>
> *on the handles of the bolt.*

I opened for my beloved, but my beloved had left;

>*he was gone. My heart sank at his departure.*

>*I looked for him but did not find him.*

>*I called him but he did not answer.*

The watchmen found me as they made their

>*rounds in the city. They beat me, they bruised me;*

>*they took away my cloak, those watchmen of the walls!*

—Song of Solomon 5:2-7

Custom required newly wedded couples to observe a period of separation. It provided time for reflection on the new life they were about to begin. It placed restraint on passion and served to deepen reverence for the act of consummation.

In compliance with this custom, the bridegroom has departed, leaving the bride alone in the bridal chamber. Left alone, her mind lingers on thoughts of her beloved. While asleep, her heart is full of dreams of him. She dreams that he has returned, that she hears him knocking at her door and saying, "Open to me, my sister, my darling, my dove, my flawless one. My head is drenched with dew, my hair with the dampness of the night."

This image of the bridegroom, his locks wet with dew, knocking at the door of the bride's chamber, suggests a desire on his part for the mothering he has been accustomed to. And isn't it a woman's love perfected when it becomes the mothering instinct? The bride has a woman's instinct for mothering; it finds expression in hands and fingers dripping with myrrh as she opens the door to her beloved.

The dream-scene is very tender and beautiful, with an atmosphere of holy reverence. That the bride is referred to as "sister" used of the Bride is significant; it intimates purity, holiness, in the midst of ardor which is aglow.

In the next scene, the bride goes out into the city in search of her beloved, and encounters suspicious watchmen who beat her and take away her mantle. This is a poetic interpretation of the courage of love when it has mastered a life. It gives one the courage to defy suspicion, cruel treatment, or any other sort of indignity.

Nothing inspires courage so much as love. Love is the most potent of all stimulants. No other sentiment is so powerful in its influence upon the minds and hearts of men and women. Why are men so eager in the workplace? Why do they labor so strenuously to gain success and win recognition in the world? Is it for their own sakes? Or is it, rather, for the sake of the women who wears their nuptial rings? Isn't the mainspring of your ambition the desire to gladden the hearts and lives of those you love—your parents, your spouses, your children? When the heart loves, what courage men and women have, what daring deeds they do! Love lent swiftness to the feet of Sir Galahad, lent his heart courage, and lent his sword victory. Love is the purification of the self from the heart; it strengthens and ennobles one's character and gives higher motives and nobler aim to every action of life. Love makes both men and women strong, noble, and courageous.

CHAPTER TWELVE

When Lovers Become Friends, a Lasting Marriage Is Formed

She

Daughters of Jerusalem, I charge you—if you

     find my beloved, what will you tell him?

Tell him I am faint with love.

Friends

How is your beloved better than others, most beautiful

     of women? How is your beloved better

     than others, that you so charge us?

She

My beloved is radiant and ruddy, outstanding among ten thousand.

> *His head is purest gold; his hair is wavy and black as a raven.*

> *His eyes are like doves by the water streams, washed*

> *in milk, mounted like jewels.*

His cheeks are like beds of spice yielding perfume.

> *His lips are like lilies dripping with myrrh.*

> *His arms are rods of gold set with topaz.*

> *His body is like polished ivory decorated with lapis lazuli.*

His legs are pillars of marble set on bases of pure gold.

> *His appearance is like Lebanon, choice as its cedars.*

His mouth is sweetness itself; he is altogether lovely. This is

> *my beloved, this is my friend, daughters of Jerusalem.*

Friends

Where has your beloved gone, most beautiful of women?

> *Which way did your beloved turn, that*

> *we may look for him with you?*

She

My beloved has gone down to his garden, to the beds of spices,

    to browse in the gardens and to gather lilies.

I am my beloved's and my beloved is mine;

    he browses among the lilies.

—Song of Solomon 5:8; 6:1-3

In this scene, the bride, still in dreams, is searching for her bridegroom. She comes upon a group of daughters of Jerusalem. The conversation she has with these maidens is very revealing. She requests, "If you find my beloved … tell him I am faint with love." In response, they ask, "How is your beloved better than others?" Her answer begins with the assertion, "My beloved is radiant and ruddy, outstanding among ten thousand," and closes with the words, "This is my beloved, this is my friend." These simple words express more than all the imagery she employs in describing him. Any woman might use the same imagery in describing her own beloved. Any bride's beloved is greater to her than everyone else because she can say, "This is *my* beloved."

For the man she loves, no praise is too extravagant to a woman. When she enthrones him in her heart, then whatever his limitations, to her, he is "outstanding among ten thousand."

It is necessary for a man to believe that his wife places him above all others, and that when she married him she captured a matrimonial prize. Likewise, it is necessary for a wife to believe she is the realization of her husband's fondest ideal of womanhood. All the glamour and happiness of matrimony are bound up in this mutual faith.

Significantly, after the bride declares, "This is my beloved," she adds, "This is my friend." Already their love is beginning to ripen into friendship. They are at the beginning of a shared life that will grow deeper and sweeter through the years.

In the marriage ceremony, the bride and bridegroom pledge to love and cherish each other "until death us do part." In most cases, this pledge holds easily enough for the first few years. When it fails, however, it usually does so in the second stage of marriage, when physical attraction is less binding and romance less manifest. The earlier and later years of a lifelong marriage are, as a rule, the safest from the snares which take one from matrimonial happiness to the divorce court. The middle period is the dangerous one. If a couple can get through this middle period successfully and safely, chances are that nothing but death will separate them.

A golden wedding anniversary—even a silver one—is a triumphant vindication of marriage; if the marriage has lasted that long, then inevitably, a state of deep affection and friendship has superseded the earlier state of infatuation, which, naturally, was only transient. Once this new state is achieved, it is almost bound to be lasting. It is a rare thing to hear of divorce in the case of a husband and wife who have lived together long enough to become true, understanding friends. The push is to get through that middle period. Reason must be asserted, and the couple must learn and practice, with good sportsmanship, the Golden Rule. Through the days, flashes of that first stage of romance may give tone and fragrance to the relationship, but only a mutual sense of obligation and a spirit of cooperation will ensure the continued success of the relationship. A husband and wife should try to look at things through each other's eyes, and then go on to follow the Golden Rule in their relations with each other—this will help them through the valleys and bring them to the stage in which love flowers into a beautiful and lasting friendship. Whatever may have happened to them along the way, for better or worse; no matter what changes they have undergone, though time has made its mark upon their features; each in the eyes of the other will still be "outstanding among ten thousand."

CHAPTER THIRTEEN
Don't Forget Why You Chose Each Other above All Others

He

You are as beautiful as Tirzah, my darling,

> *as lovely as Jerusalem, as majestic as troops with banners.*

Turn your eyes from me; they overwhelm me.

Your hair is like a flock of goats descending from Gilead.

Your teeth are like a flock of sheep coming up from

> *the washing. Each has its twin, not one of them is missing.*

Your temples behind your veil are like the halves of a pomegranate.

Sixty queens there may be, and eighty concubines,

> *and virgins beyond number;*

but my dove, my perfect one, is unique, the only daughter

    of her mother, the favorite of the one who bore her.

The young women saw her and called her blessed; the queens

    and concubines praised her.

Friends

Who is this that appears like the dawn, fair as the moon, bright as

    the sun, majestic as the stars in procession?

He

I went down to the grove of nut trees to look at the new growth

    in the valley, to see if the vines had budded

    or the pomegranates were in bloom.

Before I realized it, my desire set me among the

    royal chariots of my people.

Friends

Come back, come back, O Shulammite;

    come back, come back, that we may gaze on you!

He

Why would you gaze on the Shulammite as

    on the dance of Mahanaim?

—Song of Solomon 6:4–13

The preceding song is an account of the bride's dreams of her bridegroom during the time they have to stay apart in keeping with the custom. This song gives us a corresponding account of the bridegroom and his thoughts of the bride during this time. Naturally, as he goes about his affairs, visions of the bride constantly haunt him. Constantly seeing her before him, he finds it difficult to keep his mind on other things. As though to put her out of his mind he cries, "Turn your eyes from me; they overwhelm me."

On the contrary, he doesn't really wish to escape from her eyes. When he is alone, free from the pressure of his busy hours, he gives himself over fully to thoughts of her, reminiscing about their romance. He recalls the day of their wedding, and the vision of the bride in her bridal loveliness comes back to him. He repeats to himself the song he sang to her on that occasion: "Your hair is like a flock of goats ..."

In the next lines he reflects, "Sixty queens there may be, and eighty concubines, and virgins beyond number; but my dove, my perfect one, is unique, the only daughter of her mother, the favorite of the one who bore her." Over the years, many queenly maidens have cast their images across this man's heart, but now, his heart holds only one image: the only woman who has ever captured and held his heart. This is the one he fondly calls "my dove." "My dove, my perfect one, is unique." The dove is the symbol of peace, and of pure and tender affection. It is likely this man has had other love affairs in his life, but the affection of this pure maiden who is now his bride is the only pure and satisfying love to come into his heart. In her love, his hitherto divided and agitated heart has found peace.

There is something irresistible about this bride. In this song, the bridegroom says she is "majestic as troops with banners." In his imagination he sees her in royal circles, the center of attention: "The young women saw her and called her blessed; the queens and concubines praised her."

At this point, he becomes so enraptured by his musings upon the grace and beauty of his bride that he breaks out in this ecstatic utterance: "Who is this that appears like the dawn, fair as the moon, bright as the sun, majestic as the stars in procession?" The moon stands for whiteness, the sun for heat; this line refers to the passing of time from dawn to noon. First comes the freshness of the morning, just after the night dissolves into the dawn, then comes noon as the sun rises to meridian splendor. The whiteness of the moon, the clearness of the sunlight, the irresistible strength and majesty of the starry host: these poetically depict the bride's qualities—freshness of spirit, purity of soul, beauty of character, strength of personality—which have captured the bridegroom.

Finally, in the last stage of his musing, the bridegroom's thoughts turn back to the grove of nut trees and the vineyard where he first discovered the bride: "I went down to the grove of nut trees to look at the new growth in the valley, to see if the vines had budded or the pomegranates were in bloom. Before I realized it, my desire set me among the royal chariots of my people."

His people are the workers—the tillers of the soil, the keepers of the vineyards. It was among them that he found his bride. He calls her Shulammite. This indicates that she is a native of Shulam, a village in the Lebanon regions. The bridegroom remembers the day when he first caught sight of this simple daughter of the common people in that garden setting, and the impression she made. As though trying to recreate the scene and see her again before him, he cries, "Come back, come back, O Shulammite; come back, come back, that we may gaze on you! Why would you gaze on the Shulammite as on the dance of Mahanaim?" Mahanaim is a city where one of Solomon's resplendent establishments was in the charge of one of his chief officers (1 Kings 4:14). A dance at Mahanaim would have been a thrilling sight to witness.

This marriage, cemented with the sentiments expressed in the bride and bridegroom's songs, will never lose its fragrance and grow stale.

A husband and wife can help to keep their marriage sweet and happy by now and then recalling the circumstances that brought them together and how they fell in love, as well as reminiscing about their romance and their honeymoon.

Wedding anniversaries provide an appropriate occasion for such reminiscences. I once read in the newspaper a letter that a wife addressed to her husband on their 38th anniversary. "This will come as a peculiar request," she wrote the editor, "especially as we are just ordinary people living on a farm. People have anniversaries every day. We've never made the headlines anywhere for anything, but could you, will you, please print the following on your front page?"

My thanks to you, dear husband, on this our wedding anniversary for thirty-eight years spent happily together. We've had our share of the "downs" in life, but your kindness and love and our faith in God have made them "ups." It's such a joy to have a husband like you.

The editor was happy to comply with her request. It's good to see marital fidelity and appreciation make the front page, which so often carries news of domestic infidelity and divorce. That thank-you note was a happy idea for a wedding anniversary. If more husbands and wives wrote each other such notes, there would be fewer dissolutions of marital partnerships. The observance of wedding anniversaries with mutual tributes will help preserve the permanence and happiness of marriage.

CHAPTER FOURTEEN
Keep the Compliments Coming

He

How beautiful your sandaled feet, O prince's daughter!

Your graceful legs are like jewels,

> *the work of an artist's hands.*

Your navel is a rounded goblet that never

> *lacks blended wine.*

Your waist is a mound of wheat encircled by lilies.

Your breasts are like two fawns, like twin

> *fawns of a gazelle.*

Your neck is like an ivory tower.

Your eyes are the pools of Heshbon

> *by the gate of Bath Rabbim.*

John R. Gunn

Your nose is like the tower of Lebanon

    looking toward Damascus.

Your head crowns you like Mount Carmel.

Your hair is like royal tapestry;

    the king is held captive by its tresses.

How beautiful you are and how pleasing,

    my love, with your delights!

Your stature is like that of the palm, and your

    breasts like clusters of fruit. I said, "I will climb

    the palm tree; I will take hold of its fruit."

 May your breasts be like clusters of grapes on the vine,

    the fragrance of your breath like apples,

    and your mouth like the best wine.

She

May the wine go straight to my beloved, flowing

    gently over lips and teeth.

I belong to my beloved, and his desire is for me.

           —Song of Solomon 7:1-10

This scene presents the bride and bridegroom, reunited after their period of temporary separation. The occasion inspires the bridegroom to sing another song in praise of his bride. He looks upon her and exclaims, "How beautiful your sandaled feet, O prince's daughter!" He goes on to praise everything about her, drawing on palaces, towers, and the countryside with its orchards, fields of wheat, and lilies for imagery to describe her. Once, when I officiated at a wedding, that bridegroom, not having the poetic imagination of this one, looked upon his bride and simply said, "You are the most beautiful thing in the world!"

In speaking of the bride's hair, the bridegroom says it is like royal tapestry, which is purple. Purple signifies royal rank. We speak of one having been "born in the purple" if that person was born into great wealth or nobility. The bride had not been born in the purple, but the bridegroom sees her as belonging to the purple by the higher right of personal merit. He is her captive, held prisoner by her queenly qualities and womanly charm, which are symbolized by her royal-tapestry-like tresses.

The next movement of this song begins with the line, "Your stature is like that of the palm, and your breasts like clusters of fruit." The poet takes us again to the door of one of life's mysteries. The palm tree is a tropical plant known for the greenness of its foliage, the gracefulness of its branches, and the lusciousness of its fruit. It suggests the qualities of a woman that make her desirable to a man: warmth, freshness, grace, delicacy, and a sweet and enticing disposition. The next lines express the bridegroom's desire for the bride: "I said, 'I will climb the palm tree; I will take hold of its fruit.' May your breasts be like clusters of grapes on the vine, the fragrance of your breath like apples, and your mouth like the best wine." Now the bride responds by taking up his line: "May the wine go straight to my beloved, flowing gently over lips and teeth." The bridegroom's desire for her awakens her desire for him. There is no vulgar lust here, no crudeness, but a gentle and natural coming together in tender embrace—desire answering desire. It is a poetic picture of the pure, pleasing experience of conjugal love. Let any husband and wife observe the suggestions conveyed by this delicate picture, and they will discover the secret of harmony and satisfaction in marital relations. They will not experience the antipathy which sometimes develops between a husband and wife.

The climax of this song is when the bride says, "I belong to my beloved, and his desire is for me." This is the ultimate statement of love. There are two elements in it. The first is complete abandonment: "I belong to my beloved." The second is the realization that the beloved is satisfied: "His desire is for me."

Nowhere else in literature can we find words which so perfectly, and yet so simply, capture the highest experience of human love. This is a portrait of complete satisfaction, absolute assurance, and the utmost contentment and peace. A perfect marriage—of harmony, peace, contentment, and blissful love—is the world's paradise.

CHAPTER FIFTEEN
A Honeymoon Ballad

She

Come, my beloved, let us go to the countryside,

let us spend the night in the villages.

Let us go early to the vineyards to see if the vines

have budded, if their blossoms have opened,

and if the pomegranates are in bloom—there

I will give you my love.

The mandrakes send out their fragrance, and at our door

is every delicacy, both new and old,

that I have stored up for you, my beloved.

—Song of Solomon 7:11-13

This song could be called a "honeymoon ballad." Now that the couple has endured the separation period and finally consummated their marriage, they are soon to set off on a bridal trip. The song describes a region that would be ideal for a honeymoon, with its villages and vineyards, its gardens of precious fruits, and its growth of mandrakes (also known as "love apples" and esteemed by the ancients as a love drug).

"Come, my beloved," the bride sings to the bridegroom, "let us go early to the vineyards: there I will give you my love." Go forth, happy lovers; hie away to the gardens, have your precious fruits. We will not disturb you with prying eyes; we leave you to yourselves for your honeymoon. "Eat, friends, and drink; drink your fill of love." For these honeymooners, the vine blossoms open and the pomegranates flower.

In June, sweet peas, with their soft-tinted and delicately fragrant blooms, grow for happy lovers. I love them because they grew for a couple who, on the 26th day of June, 1902, walked down the wedded path together, happy in each other's love, and who have been walking together ever since in happy and loving friendship. It is appropriate that flowers should deck the brow of the bride and garland the marriage altar, for they are a lovely symbol of happiness and the enjoyment of marital life.

CHAPTER SIXTEEN
Be Considerate of Your Beloved's Family

She

If only you were to me like a brother, who was

nursed at my mother's breasts!

Then, if I found you outside, I would kiss you,

and no one would despise me.

I would lead you and bring you to my mother's house—she

who has taught me. I would give you

spiced wine to drink, the nectar

of my pomegranates.

His left arm is under my head and

his right arm embraces me.

—Song of Solomon 8:1-3

The bride expresses a revealing wish to the bridegroom: "If only you were to me like a brother." She wants him to be one with her kinspeople; she wants to take him into her mother's house as though he were her brother and a member of the family.

Isn't that the ideal? If a young man or woman came to the marriage altar saying, in his or her heart, "I don't care for your family," what would you expect? You may not like some of the ways of your wife's people, and she may not like everything your people do, but it is better to let the mantle of charity be cast over the faults of each other's families. When you marry into a family, it is the wise thing, the happiest way, to go along with them as though you had married the whole family. This means added loves, added brothers and sisters. When one is injured, they all feel it; when one sorrows, they all sympathize; when one is in need, many hands stretch out to help. That is the family relationship love creates. Out of love for her mother-in-law, Ruth said, "Your people will be my people" (Ruth 1:16).

Of particular note in this song is the bride's deference to her mother: "I would lead you and bring you to my mother's house—she who has taught me." Although she is now married, the bride still looks to her mother for counsel and guidance. As a girl, she must have been responsive to her mother's teaching, and well-instructed in the essentials of womanhood and all the things a good wife should know. It is possible that the reason she is so well-prepared for marriage and its obligations is that her mother's example and teaching prepared her.

Many young people embark upon the matrimonial sea with the idea that marriage is going to be one long honeymoon. Their disillusionment is not long in coming. How different things would be, how much heartbreak would be spared, if young people were prepared, by proper instruction on the function and responsibilities of marriage, for all the hazards and trials ahead; if they were taught to take the rough with the smooth, and to try to understand and forgive, when necessary, one another's faults and shortcomings. We have much to learn on this matter from the sacred writings of the Hebrews, to whose genius we are indebted for this matchless song of triumph in love and wedded life.

In the concluding lines of this song to the bridegroom, the bride reveals what she expects their relationship to be in the new life they are beginning together: "I would give you spiced wine to drink, the nectar of my pomegranates. His left arm is under my head and his right arm embraces me." As a wife, she will rely on the strong hand of her husband to uphold and support her, and meanwhile, she will cherish and nourish him. In other words, she expects their relationship to be one of mutual sharing and mutual helpfulness.

In the Book of Esther, King Ahasuerus is said to have sent a mandate to all his realm that "every man should be ruler over his own household, using his native tongue" (Esther 1:22). Some misguided husbands out there seem to think that this edict is still in effect. They have not learned that the tradition of masculine superiority was discarded some time ago. The Bible implies that the husband is head of his household, but that does not mean that he has the right to order his wife around any way he chooses (see Ephesians 5:21–33). The self-assertive egotist who lords over his household and expects his wife to be at his beck and call is a bully. The man who blusters and domineers, asserting authority and assuming the role of master, is not a husband at all—he is a petty despot.

The question of who will be head of the household never forces itself upon a well-mated pair. Of course, the husband is officially the head, and by law is responsible for the family, but why should there be any question about rights or place or authority? In the ideal marriage, husband and wife do not compete; they supplement. They do not contend; they cooperate. There is no superior or inferior. Marriage is a partnership in which two persons agree to pool their entire capital of love and their distinctive personalities and gifts. There is no question of who will reign—they reign together. The ideal relationship between husband and wife is described by the apostle Peter: "heirs with you of the gracious gift of life" (1 Peter 3:7).

A couple may be very much in love, but they have to learn how to live together, how to adjust to each other. They must reach the understanding that comes from together facing life's worries and problems and together enjoying its triumphs and pleasures.

To make marriage work, you need love that goes deeper than mere physical attachment. A marriage cannot be maintained on a purely physical basis. The thrill of the honeymoon will die down, and there will be less physical attraction. Wedded life is not all moonlight, honeysuckle, and intoxicating romance.

To realize your highest and best potential in your wedded life keep your marriage on a spiritual level. Family devotions will help you do that, as will regular attendance at the worship services of your church. Worship together, and you'll find it easy to work together. My observations as a minister tell me that husbands and wives who pray together and worship together stay together.

It may not sound very romantic to speak of the business of marriage. Yet it is a business, and a big one—the biggest in the world. It takes sense to run a marriage—more sense than it takes to run any other business. The practical matter of handling and spending money requires money-sense. Many marriages fail on the money problem alone. Usually the cause is not too little money, but poor management. This is a matter you must deal with as partners. You must counsel together, and plan carefully. Don't say "my money"; say "our money."

More than just money-sense, you need religious sense. Marriage is a religious institution, and its success can only be assured insofar as it conforms to the divine pattern and the laws of Christian morality. You can't disregard the moral demand of religion and make a success of marriage.

As "heirs ... of the gracious gift of life," a couple should be gracious, courteous, and appreciative to each other. The grace of appreciation will shut out the enemies of married happiness—faultfinding, complaining, and nagging. Love and happiness thrive on little courtesies, which are very important elements in preserving married happiness and keeping the home pleasant. Clergyman and novelist Laurence Sterne said, "Hail! Ye small sweet courtesies of life, for smooth do ye make the road of it."

Living together as joint-heirs, a couple must share their experiences and not be secretive. They must keep clear of concealment and the need for concealment. It is tragic when the need for concealment comes into a marriage; the entire atmosphere is different from that point onward. When questions must be avoided and eyes averted for fear they will betray a guilty secret, then the bloom of wedded life is gone.

.

CHAPTER SEVENTEEN

Beware of Love's Counter Passion: Jealousy

Friends

Who is this coming up from the wilderness

leaning on her beloved?

She

Under the apple tree I roused you;

there your mother conceived you,

there she who was in labor gave you birth.

Place me like a seal over your heart, like a seal

on your arm; for love is as strong as death,

its jealousy unyielding as the grave. It burns like a

blazing fire, like a mighty flame.

Many waters cannot quench love; rivers cannot sweep

John R. Gunn

it away. If one were to give all the wealth of

one's house for love, it would be utterly scorned.

—Song of Solomon 8:5-7

Now that the bridal holiday is over, the time for settling down has come for this bride and bridegroom. As they return from their holiday and set forth on life's journey together, the bride is seen "leaning on her beloved." That is the bridegroom's image of her, and the way he wants it; with her love sustaining and strengthening him, he wants her to lean upon him. We have seen this lovely picture so often: the maiden sweet and winsome, and the bridegroom strong and stalwart, go forth to face life in the comradeship of love. She leans upon his strength while he is upheld by her love and devotion.

Here, surely, is a true love match. How did it come about? The answer is implied in the bridegroom's words: "Under the apple tree I roused you; there your mother conceived you." He found her amidst the simple surroundings of her nativity, and there he awakened her love. No matchmaker had anything to do with this romance. It is well enough to provide opportunities for young people to meet—after that, better to leave Cupid to do the rest with his bow and arrows. Matches made by parents or other interested parties often turn out to be loveless, and there is nothing sadder than a loveless marriage.

As they start out on their new life together, the bridegroom expects their union to hold until death takes one or the other. "Place me like a seal over your heart, like a seal on your arm; for love is as strong as death." Here the poet sets jealousy in contrast with love, like a kind of counter passion: "[Love's] jealousy [is] unyielding as the grave. It burns like blazing fire, like a mighty flame."

The tragedies caused by jealousy can be seen everywhere, in broken marriages and ruined homes. In Shakespeare's *Othello*, for example, with whispered rumors and insinuations, the villain Iago inspires and inflames madness in Othello, until, in a moment of frenzied jealousy, Othello kills his beloved Desdemona, a woman so innocent and pure of love that she is incapable of suspecting betrayal by another.

Jealousy creates suspicion and fear of rivalry for affection. Thus, it makes a husband or wife intolerant of any attention his or her partner receives from a suspected rival. This may not lead to tragedy as in the case of Othello, but jealousy always poisons the soul and robs the heart of faith, thus blighting the paradise of domestic bliss.

Recall Paul's great chapter on love and read his description of love's characteristics and behavior: "Love is patient, love is kind. It does not envy, it does not boast, it is not proud. It does not dishonor others, it is not self-seeking, it is not easily angered, it keeps no record of wrongs. Love does not delight in evil but rejoices with the truth. It always protects, always trusts, always hopes, always perseveres" (1 Corinthians 13:4–7).

The poet of the Song goes on to speak of love: "Many waters cannot quench love; rivers cannot sweep it away. If one were to give all the wealth of one's house for love, it would be utterly scorned." Here is the great moral of this poem—love is unpurchasable, inextinguishable, and unconquerable. Money cannot buy love; poverty cannot kill it. True love will stand the test of all the tides of time and fortune. Shakespeare, great master of the human heart, knew all the hopes, fears, ambitions, and passions that sway the minds and souls of men and women. In "Sonnet 116" he wrote,

> Love is not love
> Which alters when it alteration finds …
> Love's not Time's fool, though rosy lips and cheeks
> Within his bending sickle's compass come:
> Love alters not with his brief hours and weeks,
> But bears it out even to the edge of doom.

Looking beyond the return of the bride and bridegroom, we might see them settled in their home. When a couple marry and start their new life together, they need a home. It doesn't matter so much what kind of home it is; it may be a mansion or just a small apartment. The one essential ingredient is love, which endures all, steadfast and lasting, for a lifetime—not merely as long as a passing fancy. Even with love, it takes time to transform a house into a home. However, if you give love time to do its inspired work, it will permeate brick, stone, and wood with its spiritual gifts, and make an inanimate house glow with the light of a home.

Marriage needs to be cemented in friendship, and it requires time to attain that condition. It is a gradual creation, a state to be reached only after two people who know the meaning of human love and, in their hearts, the meaning of divine love, have done a lot of living together. Marriage is the rock which stands firm against the temptations of good fortune and the tempests of misfortune.

One bride's prayer, by an unknown author reads: "O Father, my heart is filled with happiness so wonderful that I am almost afraid. This is my wedding day, and I pray that the beautiful joy of the morning will never grow dim. Father, may its memories become more precious and tender with each passing anniversary. Thou hast sent me one who seems altogether worthy of my deepest regards. Grant unto me the power to keep him ever true and loving as now. May I prove a helpmate, a sweetheart, and a friend, among all the temptations that trouble the impulsive hearts of men. Grant unto me the skill to make home the best-loved place of all. Help me to make its light shine farther than any glow that might dim its radiance. Let me, I pray Thee, meet the little misunderstandings and cares of our new life bravely. Be with me as I start on my mission of wifehood, and stay Thou my path from failure. All the way, walk Thou with me, even unto the end of the journey. O Father, bless our wedding day. Sanctify my motherhood, if Thou seest fit to grant me that privilege. And when our youthful dreams are realized, let the ripening years hallow our companionship. And so, may we walk hand in hand down the highway of life, even to the 'Sunset and Evening Star.' And this I ask in the name of Jesus, and for His sake. Amen."

There could not be a wedding-day prayer more appropriate than this one; its atmosphere is so holy, and the aspirations and hopes it expresses are so complete. Let any young bride pray this prayer—and let the bridegroom pray likewise—and it will bring down a benediction from heaven to bless their wedded life through its beginning and its future years.

CHAPTER EIGHTEEN
If and When Baby Comes Along

Friends

We have a little sister, and her breasts are not yet grown.

   What shall we do for our sister on

   the day she is spoken for?

If she is a wall, we will build towers of silver on her.

   If she is a door, we will enclose her

   with panels of cedar.

—Song of Solomon 8:8-9

This song of love and marriage would not be complete without a child, and here the child appears. The bridegroom and bride have become father and mother. What joy the coming of this little sister brings to their hearts! Of all the joys that brighten this earth, none is welcomed as much as a newborn child.

A baby is the most interesting thing in the world. The most beautiful sight God's eye looks upon in this world is that of a babe nestling in a mother's arms. To quote author Gerald Massey, a babe is "a sweet new blossom of humanity, fresh fallen from God's own home to flower on earth." When God sends a baby into a home, He has bestowed upon that home the most precious gift of heaven.

A father gains a new drive to work from the moment his baby is born, as well as new social goals and new moral motivations. Henry Ward Beecher said, "a babe is a mother's anchor." It is that, and far more. From the time a mother enfolds her babe into her bosom, new ideals, new dreams, and new aspirations begin to unfold in her heart. In Charles Lambs' poem "The Gipsy's Malison," a mother sings, "Suck, baby! Suck! Mother's love grows by giving; drain the sweet founts that only thrive by wasting!" And Tennyson, through one of his poems, hears a mother's cooing, "Beat upon mine, little heart, beat, beat; beat upon mine!" With every heartbeat of that little heart upon hers, the mother's heart grows warmer and bigger.

The writer Martin Farquhar Tupper said that "a babe in a house is a well-spring of pleasure, a messenger of peace and love, a resting-place for innocence on earth, a link between angels and men." One's imagination travels the furthest bounds when he thinks what a child means to the homes of the world. "The childless cherubs well might envy the pleasure of a parent," wrote Byron in his play *Cain*.

We should not miss the significance of the word "we" in the conversation between the father and mother about the little sister. It expresses the idea of partnership; they are to be jointly responsible for the child's training. The idea of partnership in the training of children and the management of the home is something many men fail to recognize. They think they have done their part when they provide their wives a weekly allowance with which to run the household; beyond that, they shirk every responsibility and leave their wives to carry the whole load. That is all wrong. To do his full part in the home, a man must share with his wife the responsibility of teaching and training the children; he must give his family the best of his thought and care.

Note the father's metaphors for the little sister: "If she is a wall, we will build towers of silver on her. If she is a door, we will enclose her with panels of cedar."

We have all seen cathedrals with the part nearest the ground finished, but the part towering toward heaven incomplete. It will not be so with this little sister. She will not be left a bare wall: "We will build towers of silver on her." Towers point heavenward, toward God. A tower of silver suggests refinement, spiritual beauty, and grace of soul. It will not be enough to teach her about the ordinary things in life; she must be taught knowledge of God, and instructed in spiritual things.

The other metaphor—"If she is a door, we will enclose her with panels of cedar"—conveys the idea of shielding, guarding against temptation, restraining undisciplined inclinations. It is the duty of parents to guard their children against undue exposure to the world's evils, but that does not mean locking them up and shutting them off from the world. Strong characters do not grow under the same conditions as hothouse plants. Children should not be left to follow their impulses without hindrance, but neither should they be surrounded with too many "don'ts." You can't make your children perfect according to some standard of conduct that you have set up for them. You cannot save them from wrong habits with prohibitive commands, nor can you drive them into good habits this way. Show your child the right way by example; show him that it is the best way, and he will likely choose it. Furthermore, he will become habituated to doing right things; wrong things will not appeal to him since they will not fit in with the scheme of behavior that will become instinctive for him. As he grows into adulthood, he will not likely depart from the good way, having found that it leads to the highest good.

Parents who seek happiness elsewhere might, with patience, find in the lives of their own little ones a happiness they have never dreamed. Thousands of parents find real delight in life by patiently watching over the cultivation of their children. You could not persuade those parents to forsake that delight for any other the world might offer. After all, the most interesting job in the world is to work with young lives. Think of the joy of developing the mind and body of a happy child! Can you imagine any joy comparable to it? Can there be anything so divine, so wonderful, as fathering and mothering? Bringing a child into the world is an act of creation. Surely, it is the most interesting thing in all the wide world to develop something that you have created yourself.

If God has given you a child, whatever pain inflicted or pleasure denied you may suffer, don't be bitter—be grateful. You are blessed with heaven's most precious gift to this earth. Remember the beatitude of writer Douglas Jerrold: "Blessed be the hand that prepares a pleasure for a child, for there is no saying when and where it may bloom forth."

CHAPTER NINETEEN
Preserving Married Happiness in Years to Come

She

I am a wall, and my breasts are like towers.

> *Thus I have become in his eyes like one bringing contentment.*

Solomon had a vineyard in Baal Hamon;

> *he let out his vineyard to tenants.*

> *Each was to bring for its fruit a thousand shekels of silver.*

But my own vineyard is mine to give;

> *the thousand shekels are for you, Solomon,*

> *and two hundred are for those who tend its fruit.*

He

You who dwell in the gardens with friends

in attendance, let me hear your voice!

She

Come away, my beloved, and be like a gazelle

or like a young stag on the spice-laden mountains.

—Song of Solomon 8:10-14

This song concludes the Song of Solomon. The Song closes, as it began, on a note of contentment and satisfaction. The voice in this last song is the same one we heard in the first song: the bride's. The speech clearly reveals ripened years, experience speaking in retrospect. How happy she was as a young bride, and what contentment and peace she experienced in the love and affection of her beloved. She sings of vineyards and gardens. It was amidst vineyards and gardens that their romance had its inception and flowered into fruition. What sweet memories they recall now, what happy associations! Such memories and associations come with increased sweetness to cast their spell over the lengthening years of a wife who has known the love and companionship of a beloved husband.

In the first song of the Song of Solomon, the bride enthrones the bridegroom as her king. Now, after all these years, he is still as kingly as Solomon in her eyes. Speaking of a vineyard Solomon had at Baal-hamon, and of the returns he received from the keepers, she assures her king that he shall have his returns from his vineyard: her person and personality. Despite the passage of time, she is still able to say, "my own vineyard is mine to give." And she still keeps that vineyard for her beloved. At their wedding, he indicated in song that he had high expectations of her, and she in turn indicated that her supreme desire was to fulfill his expectations. It is still her dominant desire to be a garden of precious fruits for him.

This wife was not one of those possessive wives who hold a strict monopoly over their husbands. She says to her beloved, "You who dwell in the gardens with friends in attendance, let me hear your voice!" She is not jealous of his garden companions. She knows he has a voice for her alone, and she waits for it, saying, "let me hear your voice!" She does not want to monopolize his time and company. Let him go to the gardens. Let him have his companions. "Come away, my beloved, and be like a gazelle or like a young stag on the spice-laden mountains."

As we come to the close of this poem, it is pleasing to see that the comradeship of this couple that began so happily still continues in its pristine glow and beauty as they walk together in these later years. Clearly what this husband and wife found in each other fulfilled and satisfied their desires. Each provided what the other needed to complete the fullness of life. "They twain shall be one flesh" (Mark 10:8) is the divine intention for man and woman; surely it was realized in the union and wedded life of this pair. Shakespeare might well have had these two in mind when he wrote these lines in *King John*:

> He is the half part of a blessed man,
> Left to be finished by such as she;
> And she a fair divided excellence,
> Whose fullness of perfection lies in him.
> O, two such silver currents, when they join,
> Do glorify the banks that bound them in …

Two things in the Song must be emphasized. They are little things, but of vital importance to a successful and harmonious marriage.

1. Whenever there is a dialogue between the bride and bridegroom, each is attentive to what the other is saying; whatever one speaks of arouses the attention and interest of the other. Common marital complaints indicate just the opposite, such as, "When I talk about things I like, my husband just looks at me and says nothing." Learning to take an interest in each other's pursuits is a great help to maintaining a pleasant companionship between a husband and wife.

2. All through the Song, there the bride and bridegroom demonstrate mutual appreciation for each other. Speaking from personal experience, my wife and I have lived in happy comradeship for over half a century due not only to our love for each other, but also to mutual appreciation. Through the years, we have sought to encourage each other by showing

appreciation for each other's gifts and accomplishments. One of the deepest desires of the human heart is the desire to be appreciated. Recognizing this fact is important to preserving married happiness.

CHAPTER TWENTY
Beyond the Voices of Lovers:
The Voice of Wisdom

She

Daughters of Jerusalem, I charge you:

> *Do not arouse or awaken love*
>
> *until it so desires.*

—Song of Solomon 8:4

This is not the voice of the bride, but the voice of wisdom. Three times in this song of love (Song of Solomon 2:7; 3:5; 8:4), the poet calls wisdom onto the scene to speak to the daughters of Jerusalem.

On all three occasions, wisdom comes to utter a much-needed warning made powerful by this matchless song of love. What is the warning? That love is so sacred that it must not be trifled with. It must not to be forced; it stirs and awakens itself. One must not attempt to "arouse or awaken love until it so desires."

This warning suggests something else—namely, that love is an emotion you can easily be deceived about. One may be deceived by certain pleasing emotions, supposing them to be phases of affection, while in fact, they are not feelings of genuine love, and will not stand the test of time. Fondness for flattery is sometimes mistaken for love. A woman who receives homage from a man accustomed to paying homage to the queenly beauty of woman should beware; she might come to think she is interested in the man, when really she is only moved by the tribute he pays her. She might be deceived by her admiration of attractive features and polite manners, and suppose that her heart has been moved, when in fact, only her fancy has been touched. Many a woman has made the mistake of getting her affections mixed up with the desire for a home, or for wealth or social position—this mistake almost always leads to matrimonial tragedy. A young man is susceptible to the same sort of deceptions. Let couples beware, or they may be deceived about their feelings toward each other. There is no greater tragedy than a mistake in marriage.

How can you tell when it is real love? If you observe the behavior between the lovers in the Song and listen to their conversation, you will see the answer. You see it, for instance, in the scene in which they are so completely satisfied with each other that nothing else counts, and there is no possibility that either lover could be attracted by a rival. You can be sure that this love is the real thing.

This may not be enough in all cases. Something might look like love, but there is still a possibility of being deceived; it needs added testing. The poet speaks of love as being strong as death and unquenchable. Love will withstand the tides of time and fortune. "Many waters cannot quench love; rivers cannot sweep it away" (Song of Solomon 8:6–7). Strong as death, love says: "Where you go I will go, and where you stay I will stay. Your people will be my people and your God my God. Where you die I will die, and there I will be buried. May the Lord deal with me, be it ever so severely, if even death separates you and me" (Ruth 1:16 –17).

Love can be tested along these lines. If you have plumbed your heart deeply enough to be sure that what you feel as love measures up to these statements of commitment, you can be sure that love is the genuine sentiment.

Most young people are eager for love. They look forward to mating, but they should know that love does not always travel a sunlit road; love is not a continuous experience of moonlight and roses and intoxicating romance.

A husband and wife may be deeply in love, but, being human, they can become angry with each other. When that happens, they should remember Paul's admonition, "Do not let the sun go down while you are still angry" (Ephesians 4:26).

An old sea captain once said to me, at the graveside of his wife whose funeral I had just conducted, "The wife and I sometimes had our little disputes, but we always made it a rule never to close our eyes in sleep until we made up with a goodnight kiss."

I commend that rule to all husbands and wives. Never let the sleep of night fall upon your wrath; then, when the sleep of death falls upon one or the other of you, there will be no bitter regrets to add to the sorrow of the survivor.

Actress and singer Pearl Bailey said, "the sweetest joy, the wildest woe is love." If you fall in love, you should be prepared for the woe as well as the joy.

To love another means that you must share his sufferings and sorrows, that you must weep with him when he weeps. True love does not shrink from tears. Indeed, in the hour of sorrow and weeping, love rises to its supreme perfection.

Love glows in life's happy hours, but it shines brightest in times of trouble. A line from Scott's "The Lady of het Lake" expresses this thought beautifully: "The rose is sweetest washed with morning dew, and love is loveliest when embalmed in tears."

The daughters of Jerusalem are charged, "do not arouse or awaken love until it so desires." This does not mean that love should be stifled or shunned. It is our nature to love, and he who shuns love is a poor sort of human. We do not congratulate such a person—we pity him.

All well-adjusted human beings agree with the sentiment expressed in this well-known verse by Richard Monckton Milnes:

> He who for love hath undergone
> The worst that can befall,
> Is happier thousandfold than one
> Who never loved at all.

As every rosebush has its piercing thorns, so the flower of love has thorns that pierce the heart with many pains and sorrows—and yet, it is the sweetest flower that grows in the garden of the human heart. Love is the one thing that makes life, with all its woe and bitterness, good, sweet, and beautiful.

I have had the honor of officiating at many weddings. Upon concluding a ceremony, I always wanted to say something worthwhile to the bride and bridegroom, but when the moment came, I could only say, "God bless you." It was the one thing that seemed to come naturally. I invariably noticed responsive expressions upon the faces of the couple, glistening tears mingled with their smiles—then I felt that I had said just the right thing.

Now, in concluding this volume, I wish to repeat that benediction. To all couples who read this, be they newly wedded or approaching their wedding day, I say with all my heart: God bless you.

NOTES & THOUGHTS

_____

_____

_____

_____

_____

_____

_____

_____

_____

_____

_____

_____

_____

CPSIA information can be obtained at www.ICGtesting.com
Printed in the USA
BVOW031709010213

312181BV00001B/2/P